Contents

Meet the Giraffe Family 7
Built for Greatness 8
Life on the African Savanna 11
Amazing Adaptations 12
What Do Giraffes Eat? 15
Life in the Tower 16
On the Move 19
A Day in the Life 20
Mating and Birth 23
Growing Up Giraffe 24
Guardians of the Savanna 27
Natural Predators 28
Challenges and Threats 31
Life Span and Population 32
The Future for Giraffes 35
Test Your Giraffe Knowledge! 36
STEM Challenge: Think Like a Scientist! 37
Word Search 38
Glossary 39
Resources and References 40
Index 41

Fun Fact: A giraffe's blood pressure is about twice as high as a human's—necessary to pump blood all the way up that long neck to the brain!

GIRAFFE

Dylanna Press

Copyright © 2025 Author: Tyler Grady

All rights reserved. No part of this publication may be reproduced, stored in a retrieval system, or transmitted by any means, including electronic, mechanical, photocopying, or otherwise, without prior written permission of the publisher.

Although the publisher has taken all reasonable care in the preparation of this book, we make no warranty about the accuracy or completeness of its content and, to the maximum extent permitted, disclaim all liability arising from its use.

Trademarks: Dylanna Press is a registered trademark of Dylanna Publishing, Inc. and may not be used without written permission.

ISBN: 9781647904296 (paperback)
ISBN: 9781647904579 (hardcover)
Publisher: Dylanna Publishing, Inc.

For information about special discounts for bulk purchases, please contact:
orders@dyannapublishing.com
Dylanna Publishing, Inc.
www.dylannapublishing.com

Meet the Giraffe Family

WHOOOOSH! The tall grass sways as something enormous moves through it. Look up, way, way up, and you'll see a gentle face gazing down from nearly 20 feet in the air. Long eyelashes blink slowly. A purple tongue curls around the branch of an acacia tree, stripping leaves with a graceful twist. Welcome to the African savanna, where the world's tallest animals reign supreme!

Giraffes are the skyscrapers of the animal kingdom. These towering herbivores roam the savannas, woodlands, and grasslands of sub-Saharan Africa, their distinctive spotted coats standing out against golden grasses and green trees.

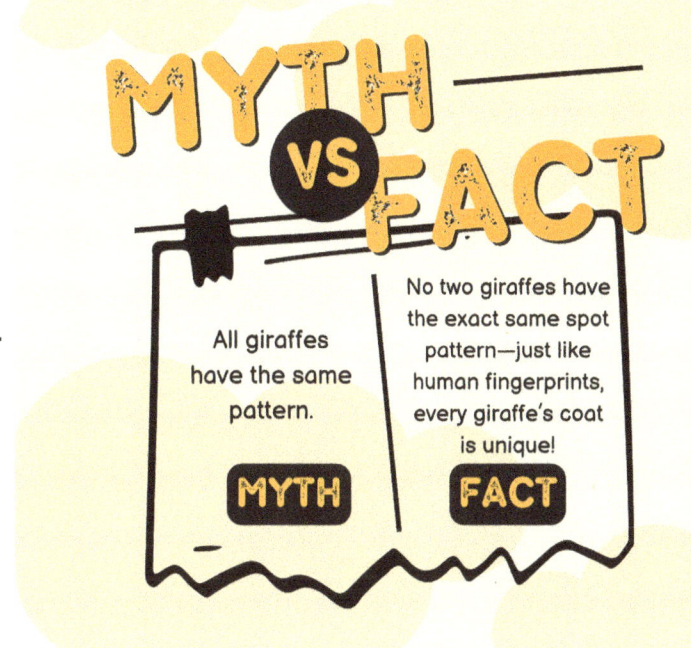

Their scientific name is *Giraffa camelopardalis*, which means "one who walks quickly, a camel marked like a leopard." Ancient Romans thought giraffes were a mix between camels and leopards because of their unusual appearance! Giraffes belong to the *Giraffidae* family, which they share with just one other living species—their shy forest cousin, the okapi.

There are four giraffe species, each with unique markings: **Masai giraffes** have jagged, star-shaped spots; **reticulated giraffes** feature well-defined white lines separating orange-brown patches; **northern giraffes** have irregular spots that stop at their legs; and **southern giraffes** have patterns extending to their hooves.

For centuries, giraffes have fascinated humans, appearing in ancient Egyptian art, inspiring African folktales, and captivating visitors to royal courts. Today, scientists continue to uncover surprising facts about their complex social lives, secret communication methods, and remarkable intelligence.

Built for Greatness

It's hard to miss a giraffe! These magnificent animals have some of the most unique features in the animal kingdom. Adults stand 14 to 19 feet (4.3 to 5.8 meters) tall, with males typically taller than females. Their long legs and necks make them as tall as a two-story building! Males weigh 2,400 to 3,000 pounds (1,100 to 1,400 kg), while females are slightly smaller.

Their long necks, stretching up to 6 feet (1.8 meters), allow them to reach leaves that other animals can't. Despite their length, giraffes have only seven vertebrae in their necks—the same as humans—but each bone is massive!

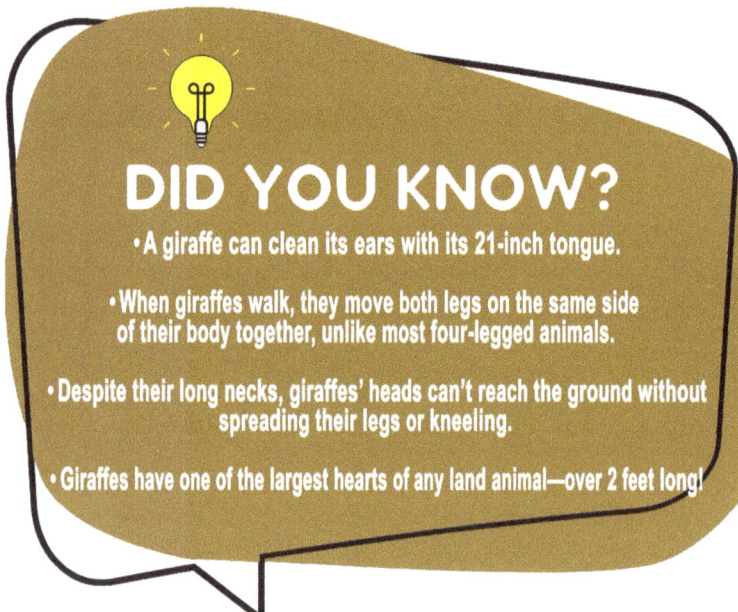

DID YOU KNOW?
- A giraffe can clean its ears with its 21-inch tongue.
- When giraffes walk, they move both legs on the same side of their body together, unlike most four-legged animals.
- Despite their long necks, giraffes' heads can't reach the ground without spreading their legs or kneeling.
- Giraffes have one of the largest hearts of any land animal—over 2 feet long!

Giraffes' tongues can extend up to 21 inches (53 cm) and are bluish-purple, helping protect them from sunburn while feeding on thorny branches.

Their powerful legs allow them to walk long distances with ease and deliver kicks strong enough to fend off predators.

Those two horn-like knobs on their heads are called ossicones and are actually made of cartilage covered with skin and fur. Both male and female giraffes have them, though males' ossicones are usually thicker and more pronounced.

With their large eyes and excellent vision, giraffes can spot danger from far away. Their unique spotted coats help them blend into their environment, providing natural camouflage.

Fun Fact: A giraffe's lungs can hold about 12 gallons (55 liters) of air—that's like breathing in 12 milk jugs at once!

Fun Fact: Giraffes can close their nostrils completely to keep out dust and sand during windstorms.

Life on the African Savanna

Giraffes are native to Africa, where they roam the wide-open savannas, grasslands, and woodlands, where they can easily find their favorite food—leaves from tall trees! Historically, giraffes roamed even more widely, but habitat loss and human activity have reduced their range.

Different giraffe species are found in different regions. Masai giraffes live in the woodlands of Kenya and Tanzania, while reticulated giraffes prefer the open, dry landscapes of northern Kenya and Somalia. Southern giraffes are spread across Namibia, Botswana, and South Africa, and northern giraffes can be found in scattered populations across Niger, Chad, and Sudan.

Giraffes live in savannas and open woodlands across parts of Africa.

Giraffes have adapted to survive in hot and dry environments, where temperatures can rise above 100°F (38°C). They don't need to drink water every day because they get most of their moisture from the leaves they eat. Their long necks allow them to reach the freshest leaves at the tops of trees, and their spotted coats provide natural camouflage in the dappled light of their habitat.

Despite their towering height, giraffes are graceful movers, able to walk long distances in search of food. They can gallop at speeds of up to 35 miles per hour (56 km/h) for short bursts and use their long, sturdy legs to wade through rivers or navigate rocky terrain. They avoid dense forests where their height would make movement difficult. Instead, they stick to open areas where they can see predators coming from far away.

Amazing Adaptations

Giraffes have developed several remarkable physical adaptations that make them perfectly suited to life on the African savanna.

- **Sky-High Neck**: A giraffe's neck has strong ligaments that hold up its weight, like special ropes that support a heavy structure. Their neck bones grew longer over thousands of years of evolution, helping them reach leaves that other animals can't get to.

- **Super-Strong Heart:** Because a giraffe's brain is so high above its heart, it needs an extra-powerful heart to pump blood up its long neck. Their heart is about 2 feet (60 cm) long and weighs around 25 pounds (11 kg)—one of the largest hearts of any land animal!

- **Balancing Act:** A giraffe's long tail—which can be over 3 feet (1 meter) long—helps it swat away flies and maintain balance while moving.

- **Powerful Kick:** A giraffe's strong legs can deliver a kick powerful enough to kill a lion! Their sharp hooves, which can be as big as a dinner plate, also help them defend themselves from predators.

- **Tough Tongue:** Their long, prehensile (gripping) tongue can extend up to 21 inches and is tough enough to handle thorny acacia branches. Its bluish-purple color helps protect it from sunburn during hours of feeding in the hot sun.

- **Spotted Camouflage:** Each giraffe's spotted pattern is completely unique. Their spots help them blend into the dappled sunlight of trees and bushes, making it harder for predators to spot them.

- **Built for Speed:** Giraffes may look slow, but they can run up to 35 miles per hour (56 km/h) in short bursts. Their long legs allow them to cover great distances quickly, making them surprisingly fast for their size.

- **Efficient Digestion:** Giraffes have four stomach chambers that efficiently process tough plant material. This system lets them extract the maximum nutrition from the leaves they eat.

- **Built-In Watchtower:** Their height gives giraffes an excellent view of their surroundings, making them the first to spot approaching predators. Other savanna animals often rely on giraffes as living lookout towers!

Thanks to these amazing adaptations, giraffes are perfectly designed for their unique lifestyle. They aren't just tall—they're one of nature's most specialized and remarkable creatures.

Fun Fact: Special valves in a giraffe's neck help control blood flow when it bends down.

Fun Fact: A giraffe produces about 20 gallons (75 liters) of saliva every day to help coat and protect its mouth from thorns!

What Do Giraffes Eat?

Giraffes are some of the world's most specialized plant eaters. These towering herbivores spend up to 16 hours a day browsing for food and can eat around 75 pounds (34 kg) of leaves daily!

Giraffes mostly eat the leaves, shoots, and flowers of trees and bushes. Their favorites come from acacia trees, which have sharp thorns. Luckily, giraffes have long, tough tongues and thick lips that help them strip leaves without getting poked. Their tongues even have a special coating to protect them from thorns! They also enjoy eating from mimosa and wild apricot trees, along with various shrubs and vines. Giraffes select the most nutritious leaves by testing their taste and smell.

Because giraffes are so tall, they can reach food that most other animals can't, giving them an advantage in the savanna. However, they also eat lower-hanging leaves and occasionally nibble on fruits and flowers when they are available.

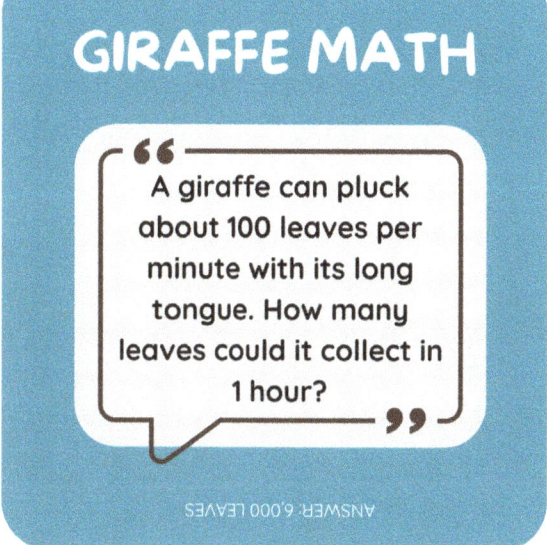

GIRAFFE MATH

" A giraffe can pluck about 100 leaves per minute with its long tongue. How many leaves could it collect in 1 hour? "

ANSWER: 6,000 LEAVES

Giraffes have special adaptations to help them digest their leafy diet. Their 32 teeth include large molars in the back of their mouths that grind tough plant material. Their four-chambered stomach (similar to a cow's) contains special bacteria that help break down the tough plant fibers. After swallowing their food, they regurgitate it as cud, chew it again, and swallow it once more—this process allows them to get the maximum nutrition from their food.

Although giraffes get most of their moisture from the leaves they eat, they do drink water when it's available. When they do drink, they must spread their legs wide and lower their long necks to reach the water—making them vulnerable to predators.

Their eating habits also help shape the savanna landscape. As they feed, they prune trees, helping new growth and shaping the landscape. This creates space for new plants to grow, benefiting other animals in the ecosystem.

Life in the Tower

Giraffes are social animals that live in loose, ever-changing groups called towers. These groups can range from just a few individuals to over 20 at a time. Instead of staying in the same herd for life, giraffes form flexible social bonds, coming and going as they please.

Female giraffes, called cows, tend to stay in groups with other females and their young. Sometimes, multiple mothers form a nursery group, where they take turns watching over each other's calves. This allows the young giraffes to rest and play while their mothers browse for food.

Male giraffes, called bulls, often live alone or form small groups with other males. They sometimes engage in "necking" battles, where they swing their long necks and heads against each other to test their strength. These battles help determine dominance, but they rarely lead to serious injuries. The strongest bulls earn the right to mate. Older males generally spend most of their time alone, joining groups only when females are ready to mate.

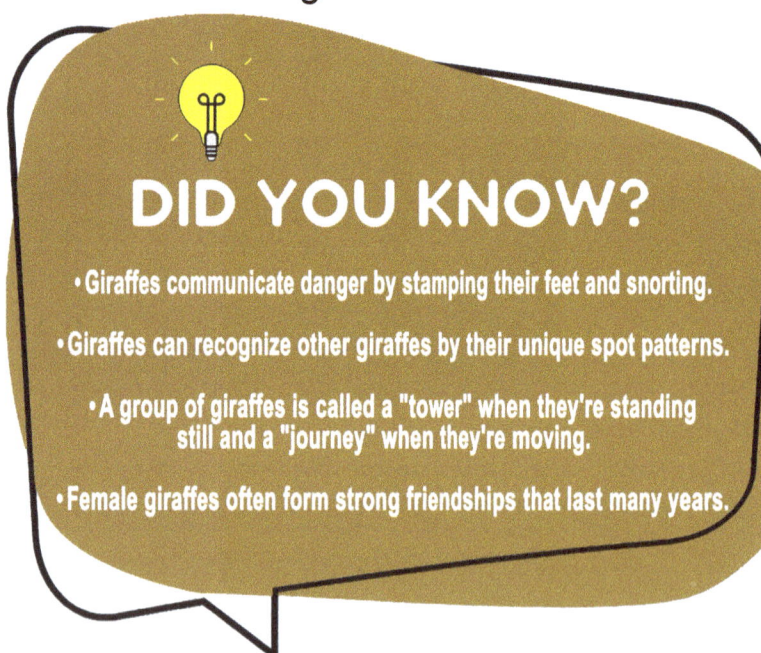

DID YOU KNOW?

- Giraffes communicate danger by stamping their feet and snorting.
- Giraffes can recognize other giraffes by their unique spot patterns.
- A group of giraffes is called a "tower" when they're standing still and a "journey" when they're moving.
- Female giraffes often form strong friendships that last many years.

Though they may seem quiet, giraffes do communicate with each other. They make low humming sounds at night, grunt or snort when alarmed, and use body language such as neck movements, tail flicks, and leg stances to express themselves.

Young giraffes, called calves, are playful and energetic. They chase each other, gallop in circles, and practice their kicking skills, which helps them develop strength and coordination. When danger is near, adult giraffes stay alert, using their height and sharp eyesight to spot predators from far away. If needed, they will run at high speeds or use their powerful legs to defend themselves.

Even though giraffe groups are always changing, they recognize and remember each other, forming connections that help them navigate life in the wild.

Fun Fact: Giraffes form "babysitting" arrangements where one female watches all the calves while other mothers feed.

On the Move

Giraffes are always on the move, roaming across their home ranges in search of food, water, and safe resting spots. They don't have set territories, but they follow familiar paths across the savanna, often traveling miles each day to find fresh leaves.

Unlike some animals, giraffes don't have strict migration patterns. Instead, their movements depend on seasonal changes and the availability of food. During the rainy season, they spread out to take advantage of lush new growth, while in the dry season, they travel farther to find trees that still have leaves. These home ranges often overlap with other giraffe groups, as giraffes don't defend specific territories. They have excellent memories and return to their favorite trees season after season, knowing exactly when certain species will have fresh, nutritious growth.

Giraffes typically walk at a leisurely pace, covering about 1.5 miles (2.4 kilometers) per hour. Their unique walking style—moving both legs on the same side of their body together—is called "pacing." This gives them their graceful, swaying movement. When needed, giraffes can also gallop at speeds up to 35 mph (56 km/h), though they can only maintain this pace for short distances.

Even though giraffes don't travel in tightly organized herds, they leave clues for others. Their browsing habits shape the landscape, and their scent markings and dung piles help signal where they have been.

Today, some giraffe populations are limited by roads, farms, and fences, preventing them from roaming freely. Conservationists are working to protect wildlife corridors—safe passageways that allow giraffes to move naturally across the land.

A Day in the Life

Giraffes have a flexible daily routine that revolves around finding food and staying safe. They are most active during the early morning and late afternoon, when temperatures are cooler, alternating between feeding, resting, and social interactions throughout the day and night.

A typical day for a giraffe begins at dawn. After a night of browsing and short naps, giraffes are often found feeding on acacia trees as the sun rises. Their long necks stretch high into the trees to pluck the freshest leaves. Morning is also when giraffes might visit water holes to drink, though they don't need water daily since they get much of their moisture from leaves.

During the hottest part of the day, giraffes often seek shade under large trees and spend time ruminating—a process where they regurgitate partially digested food and chew it again as "cud." This helps their four-chambered stomach break down tough plant material more efficiently. While ruminating, giraffes remain alert to their surroundings.

Giraffes Through History

- **Gift to a King:** In 1827, Egypt's ruler sent a giraffe to the French king. It walked 550 miles from the port to Paris, becoming so famous it inspired a fashion trend!

- **Roman Name:** Julius Caesar brought the first giraffe to Rome in 46 BCE. Romans called it "camelopardalis" — part camel, part leopard.

- **African Beliefs:** Some African tribes believe giraffes can pass messages between Earth and the heavens because of their height.

Afternoons bring more feeding and movement between different browsing areas. Giraffes travel at a steady pace, their distinctive walk carrying them gracefully across the savanna. They pause frequently to scan for predators—their height gives them an excellent view of the surrounding area. Between meals, they spend time grooming—using their long tongues to clean their faces or rubbing against trees to remove parasites. As evening approaches, social interactions increase. Mothers check on their calves, young giraffes may engage in play, and males might practice necking contests.

Nighttime doesn't bring much rest for giraffes—they continue to feed and remain vigilant. Giraffes are light sleepers! They may doze for up to 4 hours a day, but they only fall into deep sleep for about 30 minutes total. These short naps usually last just 1-5 minutes at a time. Giraffes often sleep standing up, though sometimes they will fold their legs and lie down for brief periods, keeping their long necks upright like a periscope to watch for danger.

Fun Fact: Oxpecker birds often ride on giraffes, eating ticks and parasites from their skin—a helpful partnership!

Mating and Birth

Giraffes have a fascinating mating process that is influenced by seasons, food availability, and dominance among males. While they can mate year-round, births often coincide with rainy seasons when food is plentiful.

When a female giraffe is ready to mate, she signals her availability through scent and behavior. Male giraffes compete for the chance to mate by engaging in necking battles—powerful contests where they swing their long necks and heads at each other to test strength. The winner earns the right to mate.

After mating, the female giraffe carries her baby for 15 months—one of the longest pregnancies of any land animal. When it is time to give birth, she often seeks a quiet, safe location away from predators. She gives birth standing up, meaning the newborn calf drops about 6 feet (1.8 meters) to the ground. This dramatic entrance stimulates breathing and movement. Mothers usually give birth to just one calf at a time, though twins occasionally occur.

Newborn giraffes, called calves, weigh 100 to 150 pounds (45 to 68 kg) and stand around 6 feet (1.8 meters) tall—already as tall as many adult humans. Most impressively, calves can stand on their wobbly legs within an hour of birth and can even run within a day—a necessary skill for survival in predator-filled habitats.

DID YOU KNOW?

- Giraffe calves grow about an inch taller every day during their first week
- A mother giraffe often gives birth in the same place where she was born.
- Baby giraffes can outrun many predators when just one day old.
- Baby giraffes fall about 6 feet (1.8 meters) at birth! This drop helps jump-start their breathing.

Calves stay close to their mothers for protection and nourishment. Young giraffes grow quickly, but they remain with their mothers for 1 to 2 years before becoming more independent.

A female giraffe typically gives birth every 1.5 to 3 years, depending on food availability. This slow reproductive rate makes conservation efforts important for protecting giraffe populations in the wild.

Growing Up Giraffe

At first, young giraffes are unsteady on their long legs, but they quickly gain balance and strength. Calves spend much of their early months running, jumping, and playfully sparring with other young giraffes. These activities build coordination, strengthen muscles, and teach important survival skills.

Calves nurse from their mothers for 9 to 12 months, though they begin nibbling on leaves within a few weeks of birth. As they grow, they watch and learn by mimicking adults, practicing how to browse for food, interact with others, and stay alert for predators.

Giraffe mothers often form nursery groups, where multiple calves gather together under the watchful eyes of several females. This social structure provides safety, and allows mothers to feed while other adults keep a lookout.

Growing Up Timeline

1 DAY — Standing and running to keep up with mom

3 YEARS — Young males leave their mothers to join bachelor groups

BIRTH — 6 feet (1.8 m) tall. Already taller than many adult humans!

1 YEAR — Doubled in height to about 12 feet (3.7 m)

6-8 YEARS — Males reach full height of about 18 feet (5.5 m)

By the time they are a year old, young giraffes are much more independent, though they may still stay close to their mothers. At around 2 to 3 years old, males begin to wander off, eventually joining bachelor groups or living alone. Females, however, often stay near their mothers and female relatives, forming loose social groups as they grow.

Giraffes grow rapidly in their first few years, and by the time they reach four years old, they are nearly full size. However, they continue learning social behaviors and survival skills as they transition into adulthood.

Guardians of the Savanna

Giraffes play several crucial roles in maintaining their ecosystems:

- **Tree Trimmers** – Giraffes act as natural pruners, feeding on tree leaves and preventing overgrowth that could block sunlight from reaching smaller plants. This helps grasses and smaller vegetation thrive, benefiting grazers like zebras and gazelles.

- **Seed Spreaders** – Giraffes eat a variety of fruits and leaves, and their droppings contain seeds that they scatter across vast areas. Some plants depend on giraffes to help them grow in new places!

- **Vegetation Controllers** – By selectively browsing on certain trees and bushes, giraffes help prevent woody plants from taking over open grasslands, maintaining habitat diversity for many species.

- **Wildlife Trail Makers** – As giraffes move through the savanna, they create well-worn paths that other animals follow. These trails connect food, water, and shelter, benefiting many species

- **Wildlife Lookouts** – With their excellent vision and height advantage, giraffes are often the first to spot predators. Other savanna animals watch giraffes for signs of danger—when a giraffe stares in one direction or starts to run, other animals know to be alert.

- **Ecosystem Health Indicators** – Because giraffes are so connected to their environment, their population numbers can signal changes in habitat health. Declining giraffe numbers can warn scientists about habitat loss and other environmental threats.

- **Keystone Species** – Giraffes play a key role in maintaining balance in the savanna. Protecting giraffes helps protect entire ecosystems, ensuring the survival of countless other species that depend on the same habitat.

Giraffes do more than just live in their environment—they help shape and sustain it, making them one of the most important species in the African savanna.

Natural Predators

Despite their impressive height, giraffes face several natural predators on the African savanna. Their long legs and powerful kicks serve as important defenses, but they remain vulnerable in certain situations.

- **Lions** – The greatest threat to giraffes, lions work together in prides to take down weaker individuals. They often target calves but may attempt to bring down an adult by attacking its legs.
- **Leopards** – While leopards rarely attack adult giraffes, they prey on young calves, particularly those that stray too far from their mothers.
- **Crocodiles** – Large Nile crocodiles may ambush giraffes when they bend down to drink, lunging from the water to grab their necks or legs.
- **Hyenas and Wild Dogs** – Packs of spotted hyenas and African wild dogs may target giraffe calves, using teamwork to chase and wear them down.

Built for Survival

Even with these dangers, giraffes have incredible defense strategies:

- **Powerful Kicks** – A giraffe's powerful kick can deliver a fatal blow to a predator, making close-range attacks highly dangerous.
- **Excellent Vision** – Giraffes have large, forward-facing eyes that give them a wide field of view, allowing them to spot danger from far away.
- **Height Advantage** – Their towering size gives them a great view of the landscape, making it harder for predators to sneak up on them.
- **Early Warning System** – When one giraffe spots a threat, others quickly react. If a giraffe suddenly stops and stares, nearby animals know to stay alert or flee.

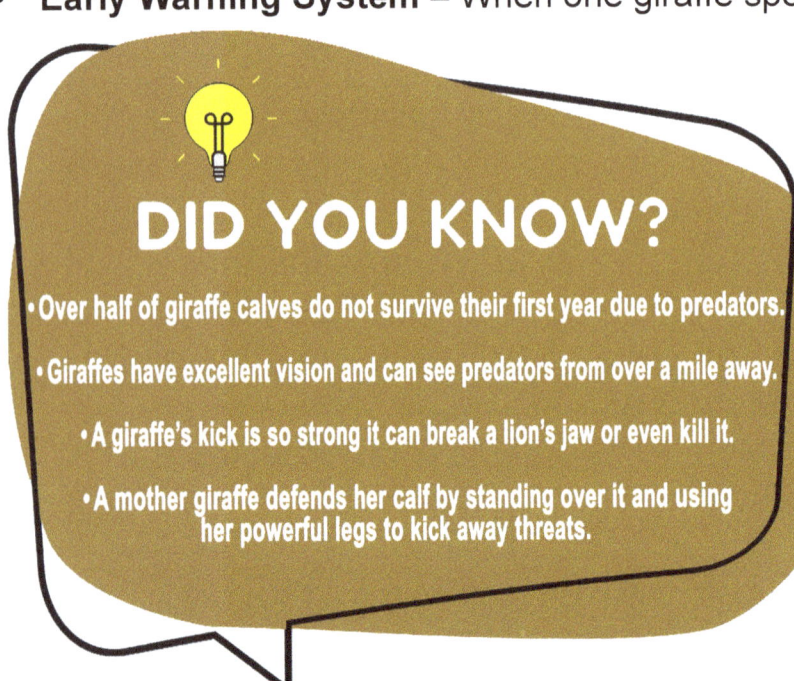

DID YOU KNOW?
- Over half of giraffe calves do not survive their first year due to predators.
- Giraffes have excellent vision and can see predators from over a mile away.
- A giraffe's kick is so strong it can break a lion's jaw or even kill it.
- A mother giraffe defends her calf by standing over it and using her powerful legs to kick away threats.

While giraffes have natural predators, their size, strength, and sharp awareness help them survive in the wild. By staying vigilant and using their powerful legs, they can defend themselves and escape even the most determined hunters.

Fun Fact: Adult giraffes are so rarely killed by predators that about 75% that survive their first year will live to adulthood.

Fun Fact: Some giraffes are now born with shorter necks due to habitat fragmentation reducing gene flow between populations.

Challenges and Threats

Beyond natural predators, giraffes face several serious threats, most of which are connected to human activities:

- **Habitat Loss** – As savannas and woodlands are cleared for farms, roads, and cities, giraffes are losing the vast spaces they need to roam and find food. Many now live in isolated, fragmented habitats, making it harder to survive and find mates.
- **Poaching** – Giraffes are illegally hunted for their meat, hides, and tails. In some regions, giraffe tails are considered status symbols or used in traditional ceremonies. Their meat is sold in wildlife markets, and their hides are made into items like bags and shoes.
- **Human-Wildlife Conflict** – As people expand into giraffe habitats, these animals sometimes wander onto farmland, eating crops or damaging fences. In some cases, farmers see giraffes as pests, leading to conflicts that can harm both people and giraffes.
- **Climate Change** – Rising temperatures, droughts, and changing rainfall patterns are making food and water sources less reliable. Droughts shrink the number of trees available for browsing, forcing giraffes to travel longer distances for food.
- **Disease** – Giraffes can be affected by various diseases, including giraffe skin disease (GSD), which causes lesions and can sometimes be fatal. As their populations become more isolated, disease can spread more easily within remaining groups.
- **Population Decline** – Over the past 30 years, giraffe numbers have dropped more than 30%, with some subspecies facing even greater declines. Conservationists call this a "silent extinction" because it has happened with little public awareness compared to other endangered animals.

Conservation and Solutions

Efforts to protect giraffes include:

- Creating protected areas and wildlife corridors to connect isolated populations.
- Fighting illegal hunting by increasing law enforcement and raising awareness.
- Planting and protecting trees to restore lost habitats.
- Educating local communities about the importance of giraffes in the ecosystem.

By protecting giraffes, we help preserve Africa's savanna ecosystems and ensure these gentle giants continue to roam the wild for generations to come.

Life Span and Population

In the wild, giraffes typically live about 20-25 years, though some may reach 30 years. Those in zoos and wildlife sanctuaries often live longer—up to 35 or even 40 years—because they receive regular veterinary care and don't face predators or habitat challenges.

Like many African wildlife species, giraffe populations have declined significantly in recent decades. The International Union for Conservation of Nature (IUCN)

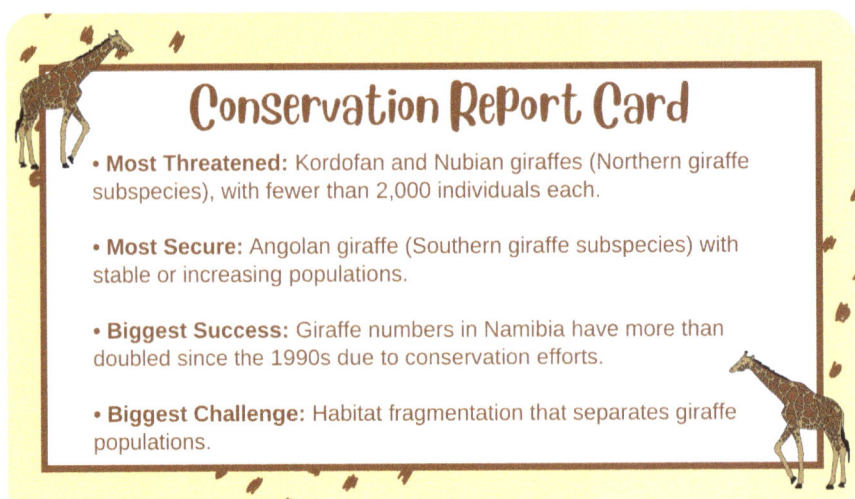

Conservation Report Card

- **Most Threatened:** Kordofan and Nubian giraffes (Northern giraffe subspecies), with fewer than 2,000 individuals each.
- **Most Secure:** Angolan giraffe (Southern giraffe subspecies) with stable or increasing populations.
- **Biggest Success:** Giraffe numbers in Namibia have more than doubled since the 1990s due to conservation efforts.
- **Biggest Challenge:** Habitat fragmentation that separates giraffe populations.

now classifies the giraffe as "Vulnerable," meaning they face a high risk of extinction in the wild. Some individual giraffe species are in even greater danger:

- **Masai Giraffe** – About 35,000 remain in the wild, mainly in Tanzania and Kenya.
- **Reticulated Giraffe** – Fewer than 16,000 remain in northern Kenya, Ethiopia, and Somalia.
- **Northern Giraffe** – Only about 5,600 survive, with some subspecies critically endangered.
- **Southern Giraffe** – About 48,000 remain, making this the most stable population.

The total wild population is now estimated at between 97,500 and 117,000 individuals. Some giraffe species have stable populations, while others are critically endangered.

Giraffes still roam across protected areas in 21 African countries, including Tanzania, Kenya, Botswana, and South Africa. Some of the largest populations are found in the Serengeti ecosystem in Tanzania, Murchison Falls National Park in Uganda, and the Okavango Delta in Botswana.

While the situation is serious, there is hope. In areas with strong protection and management, some giraffe populations are stable or even increasing. By supporting conservation efforts, we can help ensure these extraordinary animals continue to grace the African savanna for generations to come.

Fun Fact: Researchers can identify individual giraffes by their spot patterns, which are as unique as human fingerprints.

The Future for Giraffes

Giraffes have roamed the African savannas for millions of years, shaping their environment and captivating people with their grace and beauty. But today, these gentle giants face more challenges than ever before. Habitat loss, climate change, and human activities have led to a dramatic decline in giraffe populations, putting some species at risk of extinction.

Despite these threats, there is hope. Conservationists, researchers, and local communities are working together to protect giraffes and the ecosystems they depend on. Efforts to create protected reserves, restore habitats, and prevent illegal hunting are already making a difference. In some regions, giraffe populations are stabilizing and even increasing, proving that with the right actions, these animals can have a future in the wild.

The story of giraffes is still being written. Protecting them is not just about saving one species—it's about preserving the delicate balance of Africa's savannas, ensuring that future generations can experience the wonder of giraffes in their natural habitat.

By learning about giraffes and supporting conservation efforts, we can all play a part in securing their future. If we act now, these towering icons of the wild will continue to roam the African plains for generations to come.

Test Your Giraffe Knowledge!

Think you remember everything about these towering gentle giants? Test yourself with these questions!

1. What is the giraffe's scientific name?
A) Giraffa longus B) Giraffa camelopardalis C) Panthera giraffa D) Giraffa africanus

2. True or False: Giraffes have more neck bones than humans.

3. How long can a giraffe's tongue grow?
A) 8 inches (20 cm) B) 15 inches (38 cm) C) 21 inches (53 cm) D) 30 inches (76 cm)

4. What is a group of giraffes called?
A) A herd B) A pride C) A tower D) A gang

5. How tall is a newborn giraffe at birth?
A) 3 feet (0.9 m) B) 6 feet (1.8 m) C) 9 feet (2.7 m) D) 12 feet (3.7 m)

6. What do the horn-like knobs on a giraffe's head get called?
A) Horns B) Antlers C) Ossicones D) Bumps

7. How fast can a giraffe run at top speed?
A) 15 mph (24 km/h) B) 25 mph (40 km/h) C) 35 mph (56 km/h) D) 45 mph (72 km/h)

8. Why is a giraffe's tongue bluish-purple?
A) To scare predators B) To attract mates C) To protect from sunburn D) To taste better

9. What is the giraffe's closest living relative?
A) Zebra B) Okapi C) Camel D) Antelope

10. What is the giraffe's current conservation status according to the IUCN?
A) Least Concern B) Vulnerable C) Endangered D) Critically Endangered

Answer Key: 1-B, 2-False (both have 7), 3-C, 4-C, 5-B, 6-C, 7-C, 8-C, 9-B, 10-B

STEM Challenge: Think Like a Scientist!

Giraffes have evolved incredible adaptations to survive in the African savanna. Try these hands-on experiments to discover how their unique bodies work!

Blood Pressure Challenge

Topic: Circulatory System

You'll Need:
Flexible straw, cup of water, ruler

What to Do:
1. Place the straw in the cup of water.
2. Hold your finger over the top of the straw and lift it out—water stays inside!
3. Now try to blow through a straw held straight up vs. one bent at different angles.
4. Which position requires more effort to push air through?

What You'll Learn:
A giraffe's heart must pump blood UP a 6-foot neck against gravity—that's why their hearts weigh about 25 pounds and their blood pressure is twice as high as humans'! Special valves in their neck prevent blood from rushing to their head when they bend down.

Camouflage Experiment

Topic: Animal Adaptation

You'll Need:
Brown/tan paper, scissors, markers (orange, brown, tan), grassy or wooded area outside

What to Do:
1. Cut out several giraffe shapes from paper.
2. Color some with giraffe-like spotted patterns, leave others solid brown.
3. Have a friend hide them in dappled sunlight (under trees or near bushes).
4. Time how long it takes to find the spotted vs. solid-colored giraffes.

What You'll Learn:
A giraffe's spotted pattern breaks up its outline in the dappled light under trees—making it harder for predators to spot them, even at 18 feet tall! Each giraffe's pattern is unique, like a fingerprint.

Word Search

```
C C M G T E R R I T O R Y D E
Z A N E C K I N G C S G E O D
Y M L N Q B U C O R N L R F W
H O W V A R B M O I O A O O M
I U N I E D J T H W N S V S S
F F E S L S A C X N S N I S J
P L N T Y D A P A Y N O B I F
R A W E E O L V T C O I R C B
Z G Y R P I A I G A I L E O U
N E P I I S V S F G T L H N L
F Z U C Z D Z N T E A I T E L
E E R T A I C A C A V S O S S
E C O S Y S T E M H R S N N T
A C R X D U C G J X E A D U O
L A X Q G W O M V V S G D Q W
O S H D K D X Q A E N Y H V E
H F X V A C I R F A O I T T R
Q E G N A R E M O H C Z N A S
```

Acacia Tree	Cows	Ossicones
Adaptation	Cud	Poaching
Africa	Ecosystem	Predators
Bulls	Herbivore	Savanna
Calves	Home Range	Territory
Camouflage	Lions	Towers
Conservation	Necking	Wildlife

Glossary

adaptations – special body parts or behaviors that help animals survive in their environment

bachelor group – a group of young or non-breeding male animals that live together

browse – to eat leaves, twigs, and other vegetation from trees and shrubs (as opposed to grazing on grass)

calf – a young giraffe (plural: calves)

camouflage – coloring or patterns that help an animal blend into its surroundings

conservation – protecting natural resources, habitats, and wildlife for future generations

cud – partially digested food that is brought back up from the stomach to be chewed again

ecosystem – a community of living things and their environment working together

gestation – the period of time a baby develops inside its mother before birth

habitat – the natural home or environment where a plant or animal lives

herbivore – an animal that eats only plants

keystone species – an important animal that many other plants and animals depend on

necking – a behavior where male giraffes swing their necks and heads at each other to establish dominance

nursery group – a gathering of young animals watched over by one or more adults

ossicones – the horn-like knobs on a giraffe's head, made of cartilage covered with skin and fur

prehensile – able to grasp or hold things (like a giraffe's tongue)

ruminating – the process of regurgitating food to chew it again for better digestion

savanna – a grassland ecosystem with scattered trees, found in tropical or subtropical regions

tower – a group of giraffes (also called a "journey" when they're moving)

vertebrae – the bones that make up the spine or backbone (singular: vertebra)

vulnerable – a conservation status meaning a species faces a high risk of extinction in the wild

wildlife corridor – a protected pathway that allows animals to move safely between different habitat areas

Resources and References

Want to learn more about giraffes and African wildlife? Check out these trusted books, websites, and organizations dedicated to understanding and protecting these magnificent animals.

Books

Giraffes by Anne Innis Dagg (Cambridge University Press) — Beautiful photography and comprehensive information about giraffe biology and behavior.

National Geographic Readers: Giraffes by Laura Marsh (National Geographic Kids) — Perfect for young readers with amazing photos and fun facts.

Tall Blondes: A Book About Giraffes by Lynn Sherr (Andrews McMeel Publishing) — An engaging look at giraffe history, science, and culture.

Websites

National Geographic Kids – Giraffe Facts
kids.nationalgeographic.com/animals/mammals/facts/giraffe
Fun facts, videos, and photos perfect for young readers learning about giraffes.

Giraffe Conservation Foundation (GCF)
www.giraffeconservation.org
The only organization focused solely on giraffe conservation in the wild—learn about their research and how you can help.

African Wildlife Foundation (AWF)
www.awf.org/wildlife-conservation/giraffe
Learn about giraffe conservation programs and the challenges giraffes face.

World Wildlife Fund (WWF)
www.worldwildlife.org/species/giraffe
Global efforts to protect giraffes and their habitats.

For Young Scientists

NASA Earth Observatory – The Changing Arctic
San Diego Zoo Wildlife Alliance – Giraffe
animals.sandiegozoo.org/animals/giraffe
Detailed information, videos, and conservation stories about giraffes.

Smithsonian National Zoo – Giraffe
nationalzoo.si.edu/animals/giraffe
Educational resources and live webcams to watch giraffes.

Giraffe Conservation Foundation – Kids Corner
www.giraffeconservation.org/programmes/world-giraffe-day
Learn about World Giraffe Day (June 21) and fun ways kids can help!

Keep Exploring!

If you enjoyed learning about giraffes, explore other titles in the This Incredible Planet series to discover more amazing animals—from sea turtles to penguins to elephants—and the habitats they call home.

Index

A
adaptations, 12
antlers, 8, 11, 12, 16
Arctic, 7, 11, 27, 31
Asia, 11, 32

B
barren-ground caribou, 11
bears, 28
birth, 23
boreal forest, 11
breeding, 20, 23
bulls, 8, 23

C
calves, 12, 23, 24
calving grounds, 11
caribou, 7, 11
climate change, 7, 15, 31
communication, 16, 19
cows, 8, 23

D
diet, 15
diseases, 31

E
ecosystems, 27, 28
environment, 11, 27
Europe, 11, 32
eyes, 7, 8, 12

F
females, 8, 16, 23
food sources, 15
fur, 7, 8, 12

G
golden eagles, 28

H
habitat loss, 31
herbivores, 15
herds, 7, 16, 31
hooves, 8, 12, 16
human activities, 7, 31

I
Indigenous people, 7, 11, 31

L
lichen, 11, 15
life span, 32

lynx, 28

M
males, 8, 16, 23
mating, 23
migration, 7, 16, 18, 19
moose, 7
mosquitoes, 20
mountain caribou, 11

N
North America, 11, 32
nose, 12

P
parasites, 31
Peary caribou, 11, 31
physical characteristics, 8, 12
population, 31, 32
Porcupine caribou, 16, 32
predators, 16, 27, 28

R
reproduction, 23
ruminants, 15
rut, 23

S
senses, 8, 15
size, 8
sleep, 20
smell, 15
social life, 16
stomach, 15
summer, 11, 15, 16, 20
Svalbard caribou, 31

T
tendons, 12, 19
territory, 11
threats, 31
tundra, 11, 27

U
ultraviolet light, 8, 12

W
winter, 11, 15, 16, 20
wolverines, 28
wolves, 28
woodland caribou, 11, 32

www.ingramcontent.com/pod-product-compliance
Lightning Source LLC
Chambersburg PA
CBHW040224040426
42333CB00051B/3436